A Gift For:

Lori Gabriel Knapp

From:

Linda Quarneri Culyer

50/50

Fifty Fun Things to Do in Your Fifties

© 2006 Hallmark Licensing, Inc.

www.hallmark.com

Editorial Director: Todd Hafer

Art Director: Kevin Swanson

Editor: Jeff Morgan

Cover and interior design: Left Coast Design, Portland, Oregon

Illustration: Krieg Barrie

Production Art: Dan Horton

Printed and bound in China

ISBN: 1-59530-119-4

First Edition, March 2006

12 11 10 9 8 7 6 5 4 3

50/50

Fifty Fun Things to Do in Your Fifties

GIFT BOOKS
from Hallmark

Contributors

The stories in this book were written
by Hallmark writers.

Linda Barnes	Cheryl Hawkinson	Tina Neidlein
Lauren Benson	Suzanne Heins	Mark Oatman
Suzanne Berry	Carolyn Hoppe	John Peterson
Chris Brethwaite	Jim Howard	Sarah Quandt
Keely Chace	Ginnie Job	Jill Reed
Sylvia Christianson	Beverly Laudie	Lisa Riggin
Chris Conti	Barbara Loots	Katherine Stano
Stacey Donovan	Diana Manning	Linda Staten
Amie Doyen	Mike McLean	Dan Taylor
Linda Elrod	Mary Miro	Alarie Tennille
Chelsea Fogleman	Linda Morris	Amy Trowbridge
Jennifer Fujita	Sarah Mueller	Molly Wigand

Introduction

Are you pushing 50? Pushing it pretty hard? Or have you been a 50-something for a while now? If you have, you know that the idea that being in your 50s means listlessly floundering between middle age and the golden years is pure bunk.

Sure, people *used to think* of being in their 50s as the time to start planning a nice long rest. But now we think of it as the time to really get in gear. Being 50-something *used to be* the age range when people were thought to be on the threshold of their dotage. Now it's the time when people have the experience to know what's worth doing and the means to do it.

Over the hill? Hardly! That's way, way, *way* down the road somewhere. Maybe it doesn't even necessarily exist at all as long as we keep striving and doing. The personal stories collected here prove that those of us in our 50s aren't over the hill. We're standing at the summit...and we're staying there!

My Place Among the Stars

As my 50th birthday approached, I started thinking about my achievements—good job, nice home, happy marriage and family. Of course, I couldn't list celebrity, dignitary, or pillar of the community, but honestly, my ego was okay with that.

Then one day, I saw an ad for a "star-naming kit." For $50 (coincidence?) you could name a star in the International Star Registry. That's when it hit me—my name may not be on a street sign or postage stamp, but it is on a piece of plastic in my wallet, which is all I need to attain VIP status. So in one quick phone call, I secured my place in the cosmos for eternity!

Now, I'm not only 50, I'm a set of telescopic coordinates in an actual constellation...which is where I'll stay, twinkling down on future generations, forever.

View From the Top

After I turned 50, on doctor's orders, I started walking every day after supper. Usually a mile or so, sometimes quite a bit farther. One humid evening, I found myself out by the old water tower. Long past were those reckless days when my high school buddies and I would scramble to the top. Had I really changed all that much since then? Maybe these old bones could try one more trip.

By the time I reached the platform, my chest was heaving. I sat back against the tower and asked myself why a supposedly mature person would do such a thing. But as the breeze cooled my brow and I inched toward the edge of the platform, I knew. There, high above the treetops, I wasn't 50 anymore. Neither was I 17. I was just me, catching a breath of cool, fresh air and dangling my feet over a world of possibilities stretched out below.

Bad to the Chrome

After turning 50, I bought a Harley—a beauty with sleek chrome pipes that growl like Godzilla gargling cherry bombs. My wife calls it "the affair you won't be having."

That summer I rolled into Sturgis, South Dakota, for the motorcycle rally, thinking, "I'm bad"—"bad" like the other guys I was with, accountants and dentists mostly.

But on the bike I felt youthful, which is easier when you're hanging around people your own age. Most touring bikers I've met are respectable middle-agers with romantic streaks, who enjoy poetry, like this haiku:

Splattered bug guts make cool fashion accessories, as all bikers know.

Sure, you still see a few real outlaw bikers—large, dangerous, hairy people. And the men are even worse. But most motorcyclists are like me, with active alter egos and mild attitude problems, illustrated by my new helmet sticker: "If I have to understand, don't bother to explain."

Yeah, I'm bad.

The Tango Embrace

I had always been intrigued by the tango, so for my 50th birthday I decided this would be the perfect way to say, "I've still got it!" At the first lesson, I wondered if I had ever had it as I struggled to follow the instructor. But I wasn't about to give up, because I had something to prove. As I practiced perfecting the Barrida and Media Luna, I realized that life's lessons are at the heart of tango. When you're dancing, you have to be fully aware of the moment and not get lost in the past. You can always improvise and create your own pattern, or pause until you feel the rhythm again. Although I'll never win a dance contest in Argentina, when I'm sweeping the dance floor in the tango embrace, I'm reminded that life really is better when you live it with fire and passion.

Writing Off 50

acing my 50th birthday, I didn't experience dread or regret or any of the other non-fun stuff they tell you to expect at this age. Instead, I was full of gratitude. Gratitude for being at this good place in my life and for the people and experiences who got me here. So I decided to tell people about it. I made a list of the fifty most influential people in my life. Then, over the course of the next year, I wrote a letter to each of them, telling them how they'd influenced me and what memories of them still make me smile or laugh. I mailed them off, one by one, to everyone from my childhood music teacher to each of my three boys. Talk about fun! In writing those letters, I was able to relive some of the happiest, best stuff of my fifty years while reconnecting with the greatest people I know.

Picture Us Here...Or There

ince turning 50, my wife and
I decided to start hiding photos when we travel. We cut out small
pictures of ourselves, then put yellow "ticky tack" on the back. It's been
a blast sticking them in inconspicuous spots all over the country. Our
photos are in California, Maine, Florida, New Mexico, Kansas, and 17 cities
across Colorado. So far, there are 72 photos of us out there. We keep a
folder with directions so our kids or grandkids can someday find these
hidden treasures. It sounds dorky, but we love hiding these pictures all
over the place; it definitely keeps us young, fun, and. . .well, dorky!
It's nice to know that you're never too old for hide and seek.

Mastering Mandarin

At age 53, I'm back in school—and loving it. Every Sunday afternoon, just for the pure joy of it, I attend an adult class in Mandarin Chinese at a local Chinese school. It wakes up my mind to learn something so unlike everything else in my life—a different language, different culture, different history.

Of course, with a full-time career and a teenage daughter, I don't always have as much time to devote to studying as I'd like. That's when it comes in handy to be able to say, "Laushr, gou dz chr le wode gongke." ("Teacher, the dog ate my homework!")

Grow Your Own (Grapes, That Is)

And make your own wine! Home winemaking has advanced considerably since my Grandpa's first bottles of Thompson seedless vino exploded in the root cellar. Consult local growers and get your vineyard on.

You can make decent wine from most grapes suited to most regions. Granted, if the region happens to be Napa Valley, you do have an advantage. But believe it or not, prior to Prohibition, one of America's top grape-growing states was Kansas. Hence, my Jayhawk Red—a fragrant Cabernet Franc with loads of tannin and an admittedly weak finish. Hey, I'm only 53. I've got years to create an earthy, vibrant red with hints of whatever.

Grapevines are ornamental, so the yard looks cool even if the vintage is lousy. And however good or bad the wine, you'll taste your own labor in it. Grandpa told me that. He was tipsy at the time, but I think it's true.

Tricked-Out Ride

At 16, all I wanted was a sweet ride. But my first car—with no A/C, no reverse, and a missing wiper that had flown off during a thunderstorm—should've been condemned.

Sadly, I never got my dream car. Then, well into my 50s, I awoke to a nightmare: I'm at the wheel of my old clunker, tumbling over a cliff, my seventh-grade science teacher as my date. Though disturbing, the nightmare gave me an epiphany. That morning I grabbed my keys and fled to the garage. There, my five-year-old, beige sedan sat parked in its sobering, suburban glory.

I drove more than two hours to a place some buddies had taken their cars to have a little "work" done. Just as the doors were opening, I peeled into the lot.

One ruby-red paint job later, rear spoiler, 20-inch rims, souped-up stereo, and a saucy, neon light framing my license plate, I was ready to ride. And, man, was it sweet.

Vive la 50!

I didn't just turn 50. As a Baby Boomer, I took half the world with me! My 50th birthday year included my silver wedding anniversary, my husband's 50th, and the 50ths of my two dinner club friends. I decided to make it a year-long party: fancy dinners, lunches, gifts, cards, and a trip to France. Ooh la la! Fifty was definitely my best year yet. I decided, "Why cry in my beer about getting older? I'd much rather giggle over French champagne."

Going new places and learning new things is the best way to stay young. My husband and I also traveled with friends who were just 30. What we considered a busy pace was "pleasantly relaxed" to them, but we still took our time—and they'd be the first to tell you that they've learned a thing or two about enjoying life from us.

Old Yeller

Sitting in traffic on the way home from work, I often notice young people bobbing their heads and yelling at their steering wheels. It's the unmistakable sight of someone rocking out. But whenever I scan the popular radio stations, I get assaulted by girlish nonsense that always lands me right back on public radio, and feeling very old, though nicely informed. I used to rock out, back in my day, and on the rare occasion that I do hear an old favorite song, I always feel a hint of head-bobbing inspiration. So, a leisurely walk down the CD aisle now known as Classic Rock got me a new stack of old favorites. And now, when I'm stopping and going on my way home from work, it's other folks who wonder what I could possibly be yelling about (after a quick check of the news at the top of the hour).

Drama Queen

Maybe 51 is no age to start an acting career in Hollywood, but in my little hometown, 51 turned out to be just fine. That was when a friend mentioned auditioning for the community play to me. My immediate reaction was, "You're kidding, right?" But a few days later, I was still thinking about it.

Why not, after all? I no longer had kids at home to take up all my time. I looked pretty damn good for my age, if I do say so myself. So I decided to go for it...and I got a part! I played this real sex-kitten type—just the sort of thing I would've been wound too tight to do at 20 or 30. But there I was—older, bolder, relaxed, and having a ball. I'm now rehearsing for my third play and still loving it.

Earning My Wings

As a kid, I loved watching "Sky King" and imagining how much fun it would be to fly a plane. I even took a few lessons as a teenager, but eventually the realities of adult life took over and flying was all but forgotten. Until recently. Now in my 50s, while on vacation, I got the chance to go flying with a college buddy who owns a small plane. Shortly after take-off, he turned the controls over to me. I apparently did okay because when we got close to our destination, he started giving me instructions for landing. I was too busy following his commands to tell him that I had never landed a plane before. With my heart racing and palms sweating, I put the flaps down, eased back on the controls and gently touched down on the runway! It was the thrill of a lifetime! Sky King would have been so proud!

A Whole New To-Do

One weekend morning when I was 51, I woke early and immediately kicked into gear, reviewing my to-do list twice by the time I made it to the coffeemaker. As I waited impatiently to fill my cup, I fumed a little at how quiet the house was. I knew my 17-year old son wouldn't emerge from his bedroom for several more hours, most likely shuffling straight to his spot in front of the TV. Geez, how could he be so lazy?

Wait a minute! I thought. Why did I have to do so much? Did I really need to go pick up more mulch? Reorganize the closets? Scrub the baseboards? Julienne the green beans? Maybe sloth is the secret of youth.

Right then I gave myself a whole new weekend to-do list: nothing. If that's what young people do, maybe I should try it. So I did. Know what? It's great!

Getting New Kicks on Old 66

My fondest memories of the 1950s would have to be summer vacation. We'd all pile into my Dad's land yacht and cruise on down Route 66 in search of fun and adventure. We were never disappointed. Sadly, time and interstates caused me to forget all about "America's Main Street" until recently. I was looking at a map and saw that a stretch of the historic blacktop still existed. The following weekend, my wife and I packed up the car and drove 45 years into the past. Though many of the old motels, cafes, and tourist traps stand in ruin, a few had been restored to their former glory. It was a thrill to eat lunch at a drive-in that looked like a giant root beer barrel and later spend the night at a motel made up of little stone cottages. Sometimes a road trip really can do wonders for the soul.

Keep on Dancin'!

My sister and I were in an almost-empty craft store looking at yarn late one evening when Elvis Presley's "Jailhouse Rock" came on over the music system. At first, we were both just kind of tapping our feet to the beat as we shopped. But, as the song progressed, my "fifty-something" soul was really feeling the music. My eyes met my sister's and in an unspoken decision, we tossed our yarn in a bin, grabbed each others' hands, and started rockin' and rollin' like two crazy women. When the song ended, a human voice came over the loudspeaker saying, "and that concludes the dance portion of our program." It was then that we noticed the overhead camera, which had been on us all along. The people in the back office were probably cracking up, but so what? So were we! A little craziness now and then can be a very good thing.

Running With the Cows

My cousin, Billy Joe, who's a farmer in Pomona, Illinois, always wanted to run with the bulls in Pamplona. Since he was afraid to fly to Spain, his friends used Billy Joe's cattle for a "Running With the Cows" on his 50th birthday.

Using the time-honored herding technique of slapping cow rumps with a ball cap, my cousin Carl coaxed the herd to clump through the pasture gate. And then the excitement began! A few cows plodded onto the gravel road. The rest stood staring unblinkingly at the birthday boy. And three, for mysterious reasons all their own, headed with zombie-like speed toward the woods. In the end, the event turned out to be more of a "Meandering With the Cows."

But with age comes wisdom, and Billy Joe learned that while there's no place like home, you can't get your cows to run there. Later that year, he booked a flight to Pamplona.

All Dolled Up

Sitting cross-legged on the floor of the room that is my private space, I gently comb and braid the doll's thick, black hair into a pretty coiffure. Around me in a circle are various boxes and trunks of doll stuff—outfits and shoes, hair accessories, even a doll-size yoga mat. Many people are serious collectors of dolls, antique and new. But me? I'm not a collector so much as an oversize eight-year-old, recapturing the simple joy of playtime. When it finally dawned on me sometime after my 50th birthday that I could possess the doll of my dreams—and I didn't even have to wait until Christmas!—the credit card began to sizzle. I love this doll. And her sisters. Outfitted to suit the changing seasons, or my whim, they greet me every day with their sweetly encouraging little faces. Second childhood? Perhaps. And I'm going to have a lot more fun this time.

Boston at Last!

I ran my first marathon in my 40s. I barely made it to the finish line, but I got hooked on the accomplishment, the adrenaline, the endorphins. I kept running...and I dreamed of being in the Boston Marathon. I wanted to speed up Heartbreak Hill to prove I wasn't over the hill. I became an amazingly consistent four hour and five minute marathoner, but the qualifying time for Boston for my age group was four hours flat. I trained harder. I bought cute running clothes that made me feel faster...and younger. Still—4:05.

With my 50th approaching, I felt morose. Morose and old and slow.

Then a lightning bolt hit: My 50th would bump me into the next age bracket. I ran to the computer to find the magic number for 50-year-old women. Yep, you guessed it: 4 hours and 5 minutes. I qualified. Boston, here I come! I'm loving my 50s.

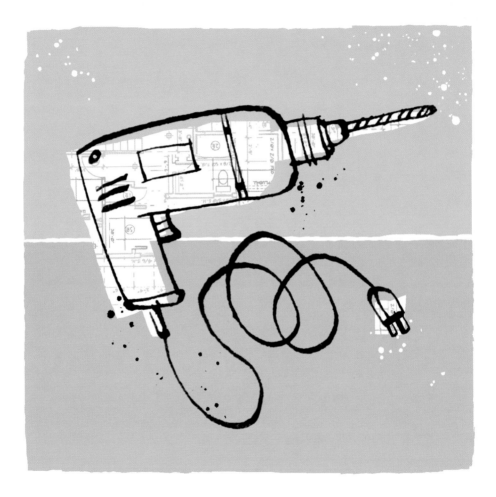

The Fix Is In

I've never been very handy at fixing things. I just never learned how, and when I tried, I'd usually get frustrated. Or injured. And I never seemed to have the secret tools required, the ones they don't tell you about until it's too late. So I resigned myself to calling the repairman (or repairwoman, a real ego booster). Then I turned 50. The truth is, I've always envied people who could build or fix things. So I checked out a video, bought a book, and built a deck (one minor injury). Then I replaced the garbage disposal (one bump on the head). Next came the dryer belt (injury-free!). And the garage door opener (twice!). The fun just never seems to end. But I have to tell you, I feel a lot better knowing those appliances aren't laughing at me anymore. My wife is, but that's a different story.

La Vida Loca

Why not become a groupie in your 50s? That's what my friend Lyla did.

And she managed to get me involved, too. When Latino singer Ricky Martin burst onto the U.S. music scene a few years back, Lyla became an instant convert. She joined his fan club, and traveled to Chicago, New York, and even Puerto Rico to see him in concert.

When Ricky's show finally came to our town, I tagged along with Lyla.

She was decked out totally in white, topped off by a glittery feather boa. Heads turned as she paraded around the arena like a glamorous snow princess. And the concert? It was a blast. From the moment he descended from the rafters to his on-stage convertible, el Señor Martin put on a full-throttle performance. But the most fun was seeing a woman my age get so passionate about something...and not care what anyone else thought about it.

Sk8tr Mom

The February day I turned 50 dawned surprisingly bright and warm, so when my sons came home from school, they began skateboarding in the driveway. Wistfully, I watched their fun from the kitchen window, then impulsively decided to go out and join them.

"Cool, Mom," they grinned, one on each side, holding my hands as I wobbled along on a test run. "Now go solo." The moment I had both feet on the board, it swooped out from under me and left me flat on my back, gasping for breath.

"I'm fine," I tried to reassure the boys (and myself), but they looked stricken. "It's okay, Mom, at least you tried," they soothed as they helped me up and hugged me. Through misty eyes, I saw the tables had turned. Suddenly, my children were parenting me. With their encouragement and my scraped elbows, I really did feel like a kid again!

Now I'm a Hoot

In my little hometown, I never quite fit in. Everyone had a nickname but me. As a kid, I launched nicknaming campaigns for myself—Spike, Scooter, Scorpion. (I liked "S's"). Nothing stuck. I moved to the big city, known always by my real name—John...yawn. But after my 50th birthday, I went back to my hometown, determined to overturn this half-century slight.

At Smitty's Cafe I ran into Squeak Ryan. "Hey, Squeak," I said.

"I'm called Squawk now. I've grown up, John."

"Actually," I said, "they call me Jack in Kansas City." Squawk turned to Sinker Swim, laughing, "He says they call him Jack."

Soon everyone was laughing—Flea Myers, Sweet Rolls Rader, Spinner Dirks, Bud Boon, Bud Keller, and Bud Hunt. But the ones laughing loudest were Snooks and Speed Peterson, my parents. "That's a hoot!" Mom giggled. And for the next hour over lunch, everyone addressed me as "Hoot."

Roll Over, Beethoven!

 recently read that the percentage of kids taking music lessons has declined by nearly half since the early 1960s. But us old folks are doing our part: More adults than ever are playing scales for the first time.

Like other foreign languages, music is easiest to learn when you're young. One thing kids don't have, though, is an adult's self-discipline. You may actually enjoy what kids hate most: practicing.

A woman I know who took up the cello late in life says: "Listening to Pablo Casals, I got really mad because I'd never even tried to play. I set up my first lesson that day." Three years later, she founded a string quartet.

"We call ourselves The 50+Four," she said. "Everybody started at 50 or older. We've been sawing away every week for a decade now and we're still lousy. But there's nothing we'd rather spend time ruining than great music."

TP Attack

When I was 53, my daughter was 15. One weeknight, she and a group of friends were chatting excitedly about TP-ing their friend Katie's house. Katie was the next in their group to turn 16 and thus, as their tradition dictated, the next toilet paper target. I passed through the kitchen, smiling to myself about their enthusiasm, when my daughter paused. "Mom?" Her eyes gleamed. "Do you want to help us TP Katie's house tonight?"

If she was joking, the joke was on her when I said yes. I felt spontaneous, excited to revive my youth—I had never TP'd anyone before! Though I may have been yawning the next day at work, I still smile and laugh when I remember dodging shadows and headlights with my daughter, frantically throwing rolls of toilet paper and giggling like a high schooler again.

To Ski Or Not to Ski

I'm floating in the middle of a lake, looking at the back of a speedboat from between the tips of two water skis. "It's like riding a bike," they said. "Just hang on and you'll be fine," they said. Just keep your life vest on, I think. Just keep your bathing suit on! Watching the youthful play and hearing the delighted yelling of other boaters is what got me into this mess in the first place. "Ready?!" "No," I think. But the boat takes off, I get up on the water (after a few tries), and suddenly I'm 30 years younger, yelling with delight and waving at the other kids. And, I remember an important lesson. When you're floating in the water, no one can see you adjust your bathing suit.

My First Recital

 have to admit I love watching old movies. I especially enjoy scenes involving cocktail parties. Invariably, there's a grand piano, and before long, someone starts playing and the guests gather round.

I'm left with one nagging little thought: "Why did I quit piano lessons?" Then another little thought nags at me: "Maybe it's not too late." But then I picture myself, a 49-year-old woman, sitting on a piano bench in someone's parlor, struggling to find middle C. It all seems too ridiculous. Or is it?

Fast forward 6 months. I'm now 50, and the proud owner of a used upright. My teacher's name is Marsha, and she's 48. I even insist on little gold stars once I master a piece. Oh, and if you aren't doing anything on Saturday, I'll be playing at her yearly recital. I go on between 8-year-old Brittney and 12-year-old Emily. And just between you and me, I kick Emily's butt.

Go Fly a Kite

There's a park near my home and on some days, I'll see several kites flying like paint spatters across the sky. Seeing this always reminds me of my dad, when a childhood gift led to so many afternoons of fun with him. We weren't very talented kite fliers, Dad and I, but that never seemed to matter. He'd hold the kite up high, and I'd run until I was out of breath, usually dragging it across the ground behind me. But sometimes it would fly. This rare event would leave us just standing and staring. I'd marvel at the kite hanging in the air and Dad would tell me what a good job I was doing. Then we'd head home with tales of great heights for Mom. I think I'll soon join them at the park and drag a kite across the ground, and, maybe, add another drop of paint to the sky.

The Pill Ching
("The Sound of Many Pills Dropping")

*A*fter my 50th, I resolved to view my meds (and the other "rewards" of middle age) in a more positive light. One morning, as we dumped our daily pills on the table, my husband and I noticed that their shapes and colors created a random design. This reminded us of the I Ching, the ancient Chinese tradition of casting small sticks and gleaning wisdom from the patterns they create. We decided to invent our own cosmic system, "the pill ching," based upon the way our medications landed before us.

His multi-vitamin rests next to his arthritis drugs? The day's challenges might require extra flexibility. The gingko biloba falls beside the lipid pills? Forget the healthy eating for a day!

Though our ritual has no basis in medical fact or psychic theory, it starts our days off on a funny and mindful track. We're happy to be here, still goofing around after all these years.

Slumber Parties

Now that our kids are grown, my girlfriends and I have resurrected an old pastime—slumber parties! We've managed to get together twice so far, and each time has been a hoot. In some ways, it's different now than it was then—nobody stays up the whole night, no bras in the freezer, no writing with magic markers on the ones who can't stay awake. But some things are still the same. We still talk about our loves, our frustrations, our hopes, dreams, and disappointments. And just like back when we were young, it's nice to know we have a circle of girlfriends we can count on to keep our secrets and who will be there when we need them. In fact, I think I'd have to say it's even better now. Back then we were boy crazy. Now we're just nuts!

Out on a Limb

We renovated the house the year I turned 52. "Out with the old, in with the new" was my motto. Then one day I remembered the tree house perched in the enormous oak in the corner of our yard. The kids, now grown, had spent hours on the simple platform high among the branches. I wondered if it was still safe—should we tear it down now while we were renovating, get rid of it before it fell apart?

I needed to investigate. Once up top, I found the open, airy little space was still in good shape. And the view—the neighborhood looked beautiful from here! It was peaceful, too. In fact, all I needed was a lawn chair and a book, and I could be perfectly happy....

Now the tree house is all mine. It's my escape on warm summer evenings, a place to relax and read and feel like a kid again.

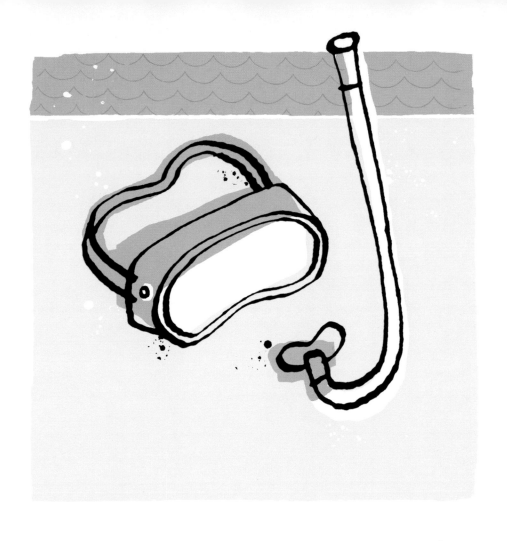

New Strokes

I never learned how to swim. As a kid, I was scared of the water. It was no big deal: in our little town in Ohio, no one had a pool anyway. But recently, my husband and I booked a vacation to Cancun. We can do things like that, now that the kids are all grown. Besides, my granddaughter just joined the school swim team. Who ever heard of swim teams for six-year-olds? And these two things have made me decide that, well, it's time.

My first lesson is next week. It's the kind of thing I used to feel nervous about—but for me, the nicest thing about getting older is getting braver. And I can just imagine myself making my way with easy strokes through turquoise water, then turning over to float on my back for a bit, looking up at the blue sky of endless possibilities.

Over the Hill and Down the Slide

he year I turned 50, our town built a new aquatic center, complete with two complicated water slides. I have always been afraid of heights and speed, but my 10-year-old daughter begged me to go on them with her until I thought, "Okay. Why not? How bad can they be?"

The two of us climbed and climbed and climbed until we got to the top of the slides. She took the fast chute and I took the, supposedly, slow one. Slow? Hah! Fat chance! I sat down and next thing I knew, I was flat on my back, banking around curves like an Olympic luge racer. Suddenly, I shot off the end of the slide I was careening down, and, for a fraction of a second, I was suspended in mid-air. Then I splashed down, creating a huge wave and came up laughing.

"Let's go again!" My daughter shouted.

And I did!

Word Games Keep the Neurons Firing

y parents turned 50 within a year of each other, and made a pact not to let their brains go soft. They started playing word games every evening before bed. It began as a Scrabble™ obsession. Twenty-five years later, their favorite is Quiddler™, in which you form words from cards featuring single letters and letter combinations. If they have company, sooner or later, it's bound to be Balderdash™.

I think it's kept their minds sharp. I pride myself on my verbal abilities, but I've played with them on occasion, and they trounce me. They are ruthlessly competitive, hilariously trash-talking word sharks. People half their age would be happy to have their wit and quick recall.

Who knew the fountain of youth could be a dictionary sitting on a card table? I don't know about you, but that's a fountain I'm happy to drink from, too.

Suddenly Six

My dad was THE DAD. Serious. Adult. THE DAD. DAD worked long hours. Don't disturb DAD. Then, when he was about 55, we kids were outside having a raucous water fight when DAD strode silently into the fray, grabbed the hose and DOUSED US ALL! A HUGE smile broke out on his face as he kept dodging our attacks until finally, I had him in my sights. He ran into the house, warning that my mother would KILL me if I got water on her floor. Then HE yanked ME into the house, jumped outside, sprayed water on ME, shoved me back outside, sprayed himself, called my mom and showed her what I had done! When mom came, he was back to being THE DAD. Serious. Adult...until he started making faces at me behind mom's back like the 6-year-old he had suddenly become.

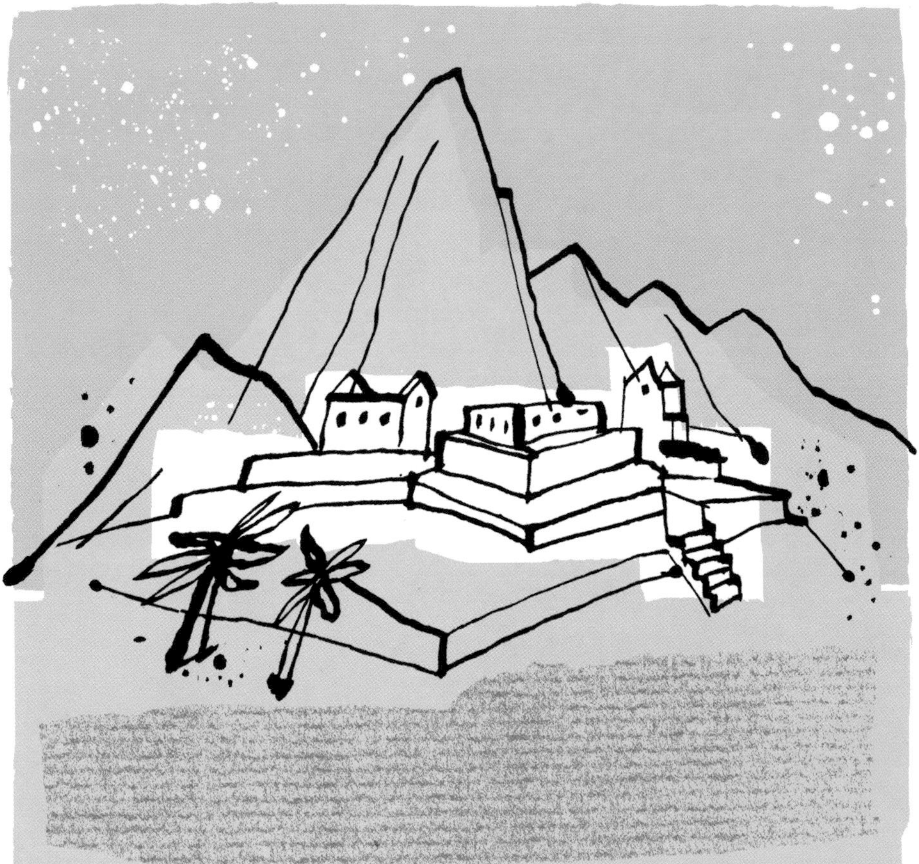

Thin Air

My friend Kathleen doesn't do anything halfway. So when she turned 50, she created her own rite of passage by traveling to Machu Picchu—by herself. She "simply knew" she wanted to go someplace she'd never been before, someplace foreign, far away, and up high. Those were her criteria. Peru filled them.

She flew first to Lima, then Cuzco, eventually traveling by train and bus to the famous Incan ruins. There she spent time hiking, reveling in the pure, thin air, and tuning in to the mystical local flute music. She found the physical space and mental clarity she was searching for. After two weeks touring other sites in the Andes Mountains, she returned to her Midwestern home. The next month she quit her job. Three months later she moved to a new city in the southwest. She never looked back.

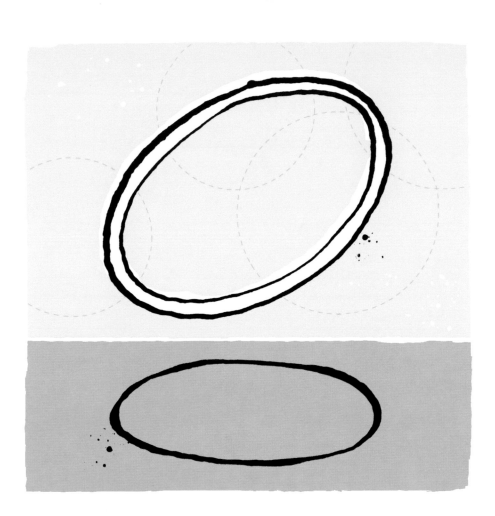

Hula-Hoops®

I recently stopped by my sister's house and was surprised to find her three young daughters playing with Hula-Hoops®. They were giggling and wiggling like crazy. Watching them with these circles of fun brought back decades-old memories. I recalled how my girlfriends and I would spend hours trying to see who could keep a hoop up the longest or spin it the fastest. My nieces were having such a great time that I decided to join in. I dropped a Hula-Hoop® to my 56-year-old mid-section and started swiveling my hips. It fell pathetically to the ground. I tried again. Same result. I gave it one last try. Slowly it wobbled around my waist. I gradually built up speed. A minute later I had that Hula-Hoop® spinning like I was a kid again. The look of awe on my nieces' faces made the experience all the sweeter!

Chasing Storms

As a 50th birthday present to myself, I signed up for a commercial storm chaser tour.

"You should run away from tornadoes," my wife warned. "Not try to catch them."

For five days in June, in vans bristling with antennae, our tour group roamed Tornado Alley from eastern Oklahoma to the Nebraska Panhandle.

One evening we stood in the Nebraska sandhills watching a supercell build, then weaken. I felt the inflow of warm air gusting up into that massive anvil cloud towering overhead. Then it gradually slipped eastward into night, sparkling as it threw spears of lightning like some old Norse god.

I didn't see any tornadoes that trip. But I spent glorious hours watching the fitful prairie sky, connecting with nature's splendor, feeling at times like I was riding up into that great engine of wind myself.

It's an experience that will last me for the next 50 years.

My Vanishing Act

'Ve spent the last year (my 51st) experimenting with invisibility. It turns out that I'm almost completely invisible to everyone between 15 and 35 or so, and I can get away with all kinds of things!

I've taken maybe a dozen last pieces of pie. I've put empty coffee pots back on the burner. I've invented and religiously supported "Casual Tuesday." No one in that 20-year span notices. At first it was a little hard on the old ego, but now that I'm making it work for me, it's great!

Once you've mastered invisibility, you can nap anywhere, you can drive as fast or slow as you like, and you can eat your lunch in peace. As they said at Woodstock (maybe), "It's beautiful if you let it be."

The One-Foot Spin

 am surrounded by little girls no taller than my armpit. The age to start ice skating lessons is four. I am 54. I outweigh the instructor by 40 pounds. Still, ever since the year I cut my hair like Dorothy Hamill, I've watched competitive ice skating with passion and pleasure. Finally I've decided it's never too late. The brand-new beginner ice skates pinch my feet, but determination burns in my heart. I wobble as I swizzle, but my inner Dorothy visualizes the glide, the spiral, the one-foot spin. Awed by my pluck, if not my age, the coach recognizes a teachable student. I pay attention. I do not whine. I try very hard. I am my own ambitious parent, repeating over and over to myself, "If you practice, you can do it." And I do.

The Good Kid's Day Off

I was brought up to be a "good kid." That meant following rules, being polite, and trying to stay out of trouble. And, most of the time, I succeeded. Then I turned 50. As luck would have it, my birthday turned out to be an unusually stressful day at work and my spirits were low. Walking home, I noticed a section of sidewalk with recently poured concrete, and I had to smile at the variety of small handprints already scattered along the edge. "How very kid-like," I thought, almost enviously, "and how nice it must be to just follow your fancy like that!" And, even as I thought it, I felt the irresistible pull of temptation. The next thing I knew, I had knelt down and added a larger, but no less important, handprint to the bunch. Oops! My 50th birthday—the day the "good kid" took a well-deserved day off.

Stretching Myself

After straining at the buttons of my too-small but once-favorite skirt, I turned away from the mirror thinking, "Who is that woman? She looks like the villainess from the cartoon movies my children used to watch."

The following day, while waiting for my daughter at the Rec Center, I passed a room of trim 20 and 30-somethings sprawled on yoga mats. When I was younger, I mused, I would have enjoyed that.

Suddenly I found myself marching to the registration desk. So what if I was 54? I added my name to the Yoga for Beginners sign-up sheet.

What a fabulous decision! I soon buddied up with another woman in the class, a lanky young med-student who had as much trouble with the stretches as I did.

Having fun and feeling great, one day a few months later, I walked by a mirror and gaped: "Is that me? I look amazing!"

My Dream Vacation

Well into my 50s, I got the romantic notion to hike the Appalachian Trail, a 2,160 mile trek between Katahdin, Maine and Springer Mountain in Georgia. I enjoy the outdoors and have undertaken many day-hikes, but nothing near that magnitude. So I educated myself about what such a journey would require: Things like the necessary equipment, how to refresh supplies, the time requirement (4-8 months, pretty tricky when I get only 5 weeks of vacation), the cost ($3,000-$4,000, plus an extra $1,000-$2,000 in gear—or roughly the value of my car), and, finally, the physical and mental preparation. Wow! My notion seemed more expensive and work-intensive than romantic. Then I realized that daydreaming about the trip had been a lot of fun and cost nothing in dollars, vacation days, or sweat. Since then, I've gone on other far-flung adventures and done some truly daredevil things...if only in my mind.

Reaching the Summit

Long's Peak in Colorado....As a kid, I'd stared at this fang of rock from the back of the station wagon on nearly every vacation we took. In my early 50s, I became obsessed with standing on the 14,255-foot summit.

But there are no roads, and we couldn't parachute onto the thing. Eventually it took fifteen hours of hiking and climbing through ice and snow for my wife and me to reach the top. The ascent was like a lifetime, full of wonder, joy, and a certain amount of headache and vomiting. So this was altitude sickness, I realized, grateful that no rendering truck could reach me.

But the idea kept me moving: You aren't over the hill if you can climb a mountain.

And eventually we gasped and staggered onto the summit—passed at the last moment by a 12-year-old girl in pigtails and sneakers, who seemed to be skipping.

River Raft Reunion

iddle-aged women? I think not! The year my college friends and I turned 50, I suggested a river rafting trip in New Mexico to celebrate. We'd reunite and prove to the world (and ourselves!) that we were still just three adventurous college babes after all! After making the arrangements, I sent "pep talk" cards to my friends, including one with a shirtless hunk on the front. "Hi...I'm Ian, and I'm going to be your river guide," I wrote inside. "With women like you in my raft, it'll be hard to keep my eyes on the river!"

We did have a hunky young guide, but it was too chilly for him to go shirtless. And while on the river, we got caught in a hailstorm. Still, we proved ourselves resilient enough to make it down the river together. To their credit, my friends never asked, "Whose bright idea was this?" Good thing I'd made us that spa appointment for the next day.

Court Behavior

Sensing that "over the hill" was right around the corner, I decided to turn back the clock by joining a women's basketball group. Although I was the oldest one there, I was able to hold my own with the 40-something moms. After a few lung-bursting, leg-screaming sessions, I was closing on the 20-some-things. And it was fun! The real issue for me was skill level. Many of these gals had played college ball. My high-school skills were decades old and not that spiffy to begin with. After an evening of particularly dismal offense, I said, "Okay, that's it! I can beat this!" The next few weeks found me in the driveway after dinner, shooting hoops. Nothing much happened on the court for a while. Then, one night, something clicked. I hit several shots in a row! And when a girl barely half my age exclaimed, "Wow, have you been practicing?" I knew I had arrived.

The Time Machine

*E*very babe needs a convertible, especially after she turns 50. The mere act of driving a convertible qualifies an older woman for babehood. A convertible is a time machine. Something about a snappy cap, sunglasses, and zipping away from stoplights leaves years in the dust, not to mention ponderous SUVs loaded with the responsibilities of younger women. My convertible is purple, officially merlot, and makes any day an adventure. It loves stretches of new asphalt rolling up and down the countryside. It loves ocean breezes. It loves Sunday drives on shady lanes. It even loves trips to the grocery store. My convertible fits me like a slinky outfit. Behind that leather-wrapped wheel, shifting gears with the insouciance of an heiress, I'm 100% babe.

Going Half the Distance

When I was a kid, I rode my bike around the lake a few times every year. Now I'm 55, and even though the 26 miles are pretty hilly, one day I figured I've still got what it takes. Of course, I'd barely ridden my bike in 30 years, but how hard could it be?

Halfway around the lake I started thinking that every little pain was big trouble. Maybe this wasn't such a great idea. Maybe my wife was right about training first.

Lucky for me, my sister and brother-in-law live on the far side of the lake from us so I stopped in for a rest and some water. That turned into football and beers with my brother-in-law. He ended up giving me a ride home after the game, but my bike is still at his house. I have only got half the distance left to cover—how hard could it be?

The Blast From the Past

When I turned 50, I decided to give myself a "blast from the past" by throwing a "The Mamas and the Papas" party. I invited all my friends—married, divorced, single, young, old, male, female. If some had never heard of The Mamas and the Papas, I would play some of their music and wait for a look of recognition to sweep over a disgustingly young face. "Oh yeah...I hear their music on the oldies station all the time!" Oldies indeed! Let me tell you that our blast from the past went on so long that everyone asked me where I was getting all my energy. My young friends left with a new appreciation of what being 50 means, and with the songs "California Dreamin'" and "Monday, Monday" on their lips. And I looked fabulous, might I add, in my white pleated skirt, pink angora sweater, go-go boots, and flip hairdo.

Reclaiming My Throne

As a kid, I was pure tomboy—always riding my bike somewhere far away or climbing some pine tree far too high. One day, nearing a 50-something birthday, while I was walking through my favorite childhood park, a breeze wafted the scent of pine my way. Well, that was all the inspiration this girl needed to climb the only pine left in the grove with branches low enough to get a good start. Despite sap streaking my skin and clothes, I climbed higher and higher, till, much to my amazement, I found the same three limbs, from more than 40 years ago, which I'd pretended to be my royal throne, complete with perfectly placed armrests. There I sat, basking among the feathery boughs, looking out across the grassy meadow below, happy to have reclaimed my regal pine...and even happier to discover that I could still scale it.

If you have enjoyed this book,
Hallmark would love to hear from you.

Please send comments to:

Book Feedback
2501 McGee, Mail Drop 215
Kansas City, MO 64141-6580

Or e-mail us at:

booknotes@hallmark.com

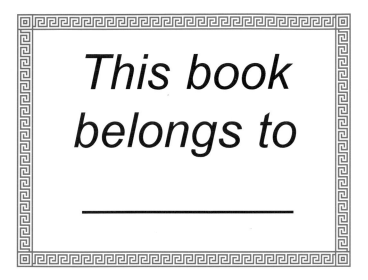

This book belongs to

_____

MY VERY FIRST
BOOK of

BIBLE

HEROES

The Bible version used in this publication is *The New King James Version.* Copyright © 1979, 1980, 1982, Thomas Nelson, Inc.

My Very First Book of Bible Heroes
ISBN 1-56292-681-0

Text copyright © 1993, 2001 by Mary Hollingsworth

Copyright © 1993, 2001 by Educational Publishing Concepts, Inc.
P.O. Box 665
Wheaton, Illinois 60189

Published by Honor Kidz
An Imprint of Honor Books, Inc.
P.O. Box 55388
Tulsa, Oklahoma 74155

MY VERY FIRST
BOOK OF

BIBLE
HEROES

Mary Hollingsworth

Illustrated by
Rick Incrocci

HONOR
kidz

An Imprint of Honor Books, Inc.
Tulsa, Oklahoma

Dear Parents,

Who is your child's hero? Is it Barney the purple dinosaur? Maybe it's Wonder Woman or Batman or Big Bird. Perhaps it's even one of your own childhood heroes, such as Mickey Mouse or the Lone Ranger.

Well, those are fun make-believe heroes all right. But the heroes of the Bible are even better. The heroes your child will learn about in this book were real people— God's people. And their stories are true, not make-believe.

Your child will like this book about God's heroes. You'll probably find one or two heroes your child will want to be like. It might be Solomon, the wisest man who ever lived. Or it might be David, who killed a lion. It might be Esther, the queen who saved her people, or Deborah, who led her people into battle.

No matter which Bible hero your child chooses to be like, you can have confidence that she or he has chosen one of God's heroes, too. The adventure stories of His amazing heroes are waiting to challenge and encourage your child. Just turn the page.

Mary Hollingsworth

Noah

The Man Who Pleased God

A flood was coming. God told Noah to build a giant boat. It was to be big enough for two of every kind of animal on earth. Noah built the big boat just the way God said. That made God happy. So God saved Noah's family and all the animals from the Flood. Noah was a real hero.

A Real Hero

1. Why was God pleased with Noah? (Noah obeyed God.)
2. Will God be pleased with you if you obey Him? (Yes.)

Noah found grace in the eyes of the
LORD.

Genesis 6:8

Abraham

The Man Who Was Father of a Nation

Abram was a good man. God promised to give Abram a big family. Abram believed God. So he did just what God said to do. God kept His promise. He gave Abram many children and grandchildren. They are called Hebrews. They were God's chosen people. Then God changed Abram's name to Abraham. Abraham means "father of a nation."

A Real Hero

1. Point to Abraham's family in the picture.
2. Does God always keep His promises? (Yes.)

God said to Abraham, "I will make you a great nation."

Genesis 12:2

Jacob

The Man Who Wrestled with God

One night God came and wrestled with Jacob. They wrestled all night long. Then God said, "Let Me go; it is almost morning." Jacob said, "No. I will not let You go until You bless me." So God blessed him. Jacob had wrestled with God without dying. He was a real hero!

A Real Hero

1. Where is Jacob in the picture?
2. How do you sometimes wrestle with God?

Jacob was left alone; and a Man
wrestled with him until the breaking of
day.

Genesis 32:24

Joseph

The Man Who Was a Prince from a Pit

Joseph had ten big brothers. But his father liked Joseph best. This made his brothers angry. So they hid Joseph in a deep pit. Then they sold him to men going to Egypt. Things looked bad for Joseph. God had a surprise for him. He made Joseph a prince in Egypt!

A Real Hero

1. Should brothers and sisters get angry with each other? (No.)
2. Put on your bathrobe. Pretend you are a prince like Joseph.

The LORD was with Joseph, and he was
a successful man.

Genesis 39:2

Jochebed

The Woman Who Was a Brave Mother

A woman named Jochebed had a baby boy. She was afraid the king would hurt her baby. So she hid him in a tiny basket in the river. Soon the king's daughter found the baby. She took him home to be her baby. She named him Moses. He grew up as the king's grandson. He became a great leader! Jochebed was a brave and wise mother.

A Real Hero

1. Where is baby Moses in the picture?
2. Ask an adult to help you read the story of Jochebed and baby Moses in Exodus 2.

And when she [Jochebed] saw he was a beautiful child, she hid him three months.

Exodus 2:2

Miriam

The Woman Who Was a Leader of Praise

Miriam was so happy! God saved her people from the army of Egypt. God made a dry path through the Red Sea for them to walk on. Miriam wanted to show God how thankful the people were. So she led all the women in a dance to praise God.

A Real Hero

1. Why is Miriam so happy in the picture? (God saved her people.)
2. Make up a happy dance for God. Do it right now.

Sing to the LORD, for He has triumphed gloriously!

Exodus 15:21

Moses

The Man Who Was God's Lawgiver

Moses did what God said to do all his life. So God chose Moses for a big job. He led God's people out of Egypt. He led them to the land God promised them. God gave Moses a special law for the people to obey. We call it the Law of Moses. The Ten Commandments are part of that law.

A Real Hero

1. Why is Moses a hero? (He did what God said to do.)
2. How can you be a hero, too? (By obeying God.)

He [the LORD] gave Moses two tablets
. . . of stone, written with the finger of
God.

Exodus 31:18

Rahab

The Woman Who Was a Friend of God's Spies

God told His people to capture the city of Jericho. So they sent two men to spy out the city. The spies stayed at Rahab's house. She knew they were God's spies. So she hid them from the king of Jericho's soldiers. She told the soldiers that the spies were gone. It was a brave thing to do. God's people came to capture Jericho. But they rescued Rahab's family.

A Real Hero

1. What do you think Rahab is telling the spies? ("You can hide over here.")
2. Put on a disguise. Pretend you are one of God's spies.

Then the woman [Rahab] took the two men and hid them.

Joshua 2:4

Deborah

The Woman Who Was a Judge and an Army Leader

Deborah was a wise woman. She was also a great leader of God's army. One day she told Barak to lead ten thousand soldiers into battle. Barak said, "If you will go with me, I will go; but if you will not go with me, I will not go!" So Deborah led the army with him. They beat the enemy! Deborah was a real hero for God.

A Real Hero

1. Pretend you are Deborah or Barak. Lead God's army into battle.
2. Sing the song "I'm in the Lord's Army."

And the children of Israel came up to
her [Deborah] for judgment.

Judges 4:5

Samson

The Man Who Was God's Strongest

Samson was the strongest man who has ever lived. He was strong because he obeyed God. God helped him. One day some men tied Samson up with two strong ropes. Then he heard a thousand enemies coming. Samson broke the ropes easily. Then he beat the enemy soldiers all by himself. He was a superhero for God.

A Real Hero

1. Where did Samson get his strength? (From God.)
2. Name the strongest heroes you know. Samson was even stronger than they are.

And the Spirit of the LORD came
mightily upon him [Samson].

Judges 14:6

Ruth

The Woman Who Was Loyal and Kind

Ruth's husband died. But she would not leave her husband's mother, Naomi, all alone. She took care of Naomi. She worked hard. She picked up grain for them to eat. Everyone knew how loyal and kind Ruth was. Boaz was a relative of Naomi. He asked Ruth to marry him. She did. Then they were all very happy.

A Real Hero

1. Does God want us to be loyal and kind? (Yes.)
2. Ask an adult to help you find the name of Ruth and Boaz's baby in Ruth 4:17.

Boaz said to Ruth, "All the people of my town know that you are a virtuous woman."

Ruth 3:11

Hannah
The Woman Who Was a Promise Keeper

Hannah was sad. She wanted a baby boy. But she did not have one. She prayed to God for a son. She promised the boy would serve God all his life. God gave Hannah a baby boy named Samuel. Hannah was so happy! When Samuel was old enough, Hannah kept her promise to God. She took Samuel to the temple. He grew up serving God.

A Real Hero

1. Why was Hannah a hero to God? (She kept her promises.)
2. How can you be a hero like Hannah? (By keeping promise.)

Then she [Hannah] made a vow and said, " . . . if you will give [me] a male child, then I will give him to the LORD all the days of his life."

1 Samuel 1:11

David

The Man Who Had God's Heart

David was a shepherd. He took care of his father's sheep. One time a lion came to attack the sheep. David fought the lion. He killed it to protect the sheep. David wanted to be like God. He wanted to be good. God loved David very much. His heart was good and pure like God's heart.

A Real Hero

1. Why did God love David so much? (David had a good and pure heart.)
2. Draw your own picture of David fighting the lion.

The LORD has sought for Himself a man [David] after His own heart.

1 Samuel 13:14

Jonathan

The Man Who Was a Best Friend

Jonathan was David's best friend. Jonathan's father was King Saul. Saul wanted to hurt David. Jonathan helped David escape from the king. He shot an arrow to signal David. It was a brave thing to do. David loved Jonathan. He was a real hero.

A Real Hero

1. Who is your best friend?
2. Read the story of how Jonathan saved David in 1 Samuel 20.

Now Jonathan loved . . . [David] . . . as
he loved his own soul.

1 Samuel 20:17

Abigail
The Woman Who Was Wise

Abigail's husband, Nabal, ws not a wise man. King David asked Nabal to feed God's soldiers. Nabal would not do it. Abigail was a wise woman. She took food to King David. She begged him not to kill Nabal. David liked Abigail. He did what she asked. Later Nabal died. David asked Abigail to be his wife. Abigail became queen.

A Real Hero

1. Ask an adult to help you fix a basket of food. Then give it to someone as Abigail did.
2. Have you ever been a peacemaker like Abigail?

So Abigail . . . followed the messengers
of David and became his wife.

1 Samuel 25:42

Solomon

The Man Who Was God's Wisest

Solomon was the king of God's people. He loved God. He wanted to do right. God said, "Ask Me for anything, and I'll give it to you." Solomon could have asked for money or great power. He asked God to make him wise so he could lead God's people well. This made God happy. He made Solomon the wisest man who ever lived. He also gave him great power and lots of money.

A Real Hero

1. If God told you to ask for anything you want, what would you ask for?
2. Talk to God right now. Ask Him to make you wise like Solomon.

God gave Solomon wisdom and . . .
great understanding.

1 Kings 4:29

Elijah

The Man Who Rode the Wind

Elijah was one of God's special messengers. He told God's message to people for many years. That made him a hero. One day Elijah and his friend Elisha were walking by a river. All at once a chariot and horses made of fire came between them. A great wind swooped down. It took Elijah to heaven. So Elijah never died.

A Real Hero

1. What do you think it would be like to ride the wind?
2. Draw a picture of the chariot and horses made of fire.

Elijah went up by a whirlwind into heaven.

2 Kings 2:11

Esther

The Woman Who Was a Brave Queen

Esther was queen of Persia. One day Haman tricked the king. The king made a law to kill all of God's people, the Jews. Esther was a Jew! The king could kill anyone who came to see him without being invited. Esther bravely went to see the king. She asked him to save her people. The king loved Esther. He welcomed her and saved the Jews.

A Real Hero

1. Make a paper crown to wear. Pretend you are Queen Esther or the king.
2. Have you ever had to do something that really scared you?

I will go to the king, which is against the law; and if I perish, I perish!

Esther 4:16

Job

The Man Who Was a Patient Servant of God

Job was one of God's best servants. He did everything right. He was good. Then Satan attacked Job. He killed all of Job's children. He killed Job's sheep and cattle. He made Job lose all his money. But Job loved God and trusted Him. He was a patient servant of God. God loved Job very much.

A Real Hero

1. What would you say to Job when all the bad things happened to him?
2. Why did God love Job? (He trusted God.)

[Job] was blameless and upright, and
one who feared God and shunned evil.

Job 1:1

Jeremiah
The Man Who Spoke for God

Jeremiah was a brave messenger for God. God was sad because His people did not obey Him anymore. He showed Jeremiah all the bad things the people did. Jeremiah cried in front of the people to show them God's sadness. This made the people angry. They tried to hurt Jeremiah. But God kept him safe. Jeremiah still spoke for God.

A Real Hero

1. Do you think God cries when you do something bad? (Yes.)
2. How can you keep God smiling? (By being good.)

God said to Jeremiah, "I have put My words in your mouth."

Jeremiah 1:9

Daniel
The Man Who Was God's Dream Teller

The king could not sleep. A bad dream kept him awake. He called his magicians and star watchers. He asked them what his dream meant. They could not tell him. God helped Daniel see the king's dream. Daniel told the king all about his dream. Then he told him what it meant. The king believed in God. God made Daniel ruler over all the wise men in the kingdom.

A Real Hero

1. Tell about a dream you had.
2. What do you think your dream means?

Then the secret [dream] was revealed to
Daniel in a night vision.

Daniel 2:19

Mary

The Woman Who Was Mother of the Lord

Mary obeyed God's laws all her life. She was pure and right. God chose Mary for a special honor. She was the mother of God's Son! The baby was born one night in a stable. A new star in the sky told the world about the baby. Mary named the baby Jesus. He was going to be the King of all the earth!

A Real Hero

1. Sing "Silent Night" with your mom or dad.
2. Why did God choose Mary to be the mother of His Son? (Because she was pure and right.)

The virgin shall be with child, and bear a Son.

Matthew 1:23

Jesus
The Man Who Was God's Son

Jesus was the most special person ever born. That is because His Father was God. Jesus did wonderful things called miracles. He made sick people well. He made dead people live again. He made blind people see. Jesus was really God in a human's body. That is why He can save us from sin. Jesus is the greatest hero of all!

A Real Hero

1.   What can you do to help people?
2.   Sing "Jesus Loves Me."

Call His name Jesus, for He will save
His people from their sins.

Matthew 1:21

John the Baptist
The Man Who Was God's Voice in the Desert

John the Baptist lived in the desert. He ate locusts and wild honey. He wore clothes made of camel's hair. God gave John an important job. John told people that Jesus was coming soon. He told them to turn away from their sins. He said to get ready for Jesus.

A Real Hero

1. Pretend you are John the Baptist. Stand up and preach to the people.
2. Ask an adult to fix you a snack made with honey like John the Baptist ate.

John the Baptist came preaching in the
wilderness.

Matthew 3:1

Peter
The Man Who Walked On Water

Jesus' followers were on a boat. The wind blew. The boat rocked. Then Peter thought he saw a ghost! It was really Jesus. He was walking on the water. Peter asked Jesus to let him walk on the water, too. Jesus said, "Come." Peter got out of the boat. He walked toward Jesus on the water. He was a brave man!

A Real Hero

1. Draw a picture of Peter walking on the water toward Jesus.
2. Read this story in Matthew 14:22-23

When Peter had come down out of the
boat, he walked on the water to go to
Jesus.

Matthew 14:29

Luke

The Man Who Was God's Writer

Luke was a doctor. He was also Jesus' friend. God gave Luke a job. He wrote the story of Jesus' life. This book is called Luke. It tells how Jesus was born, lived, died, and came back to life. Luke also wrote the book of Acts. It is about Jesus' church and how it grew. Thanks to Luke, we know about Jesus and His church. He is a hero.

A Real Hero

1. Sing "Tell Me the Story of Jesus" with someone.
2. Put on something white. Pretend you are Doctor Luke and help sick people.

It seemed good to me . . . to write to you an orderly account.

Luke 1:3

A Poor Widow
The Woman Who Was a True Giver

One day Jesus sat in the temple. He watched people give money to God. Rich people gave lots of money. They had lots of money left. Then a poor woman gave two tiny coins. Jesus said she gave more than all the others. She gave all her money. She even gave her food money. She trusted God to take care of her.

A Real Hero

1. Why was the poor woman a hero? (She trusted God to care for her.)
2. Do you have something you would like to give God?

Jesus said, "This poor widow has put in more than all."

Luke 21:3

Andrew
The Man Who Was a Loving Brother

Andrew heard John the Baptist teach about Jesus. He knew Jesus could save people. He knew Jesus was the Son of God. Andrew found his brother Simon (Peter). He brought Simon to Jesus. Simon was saved, too. Andrew was a loving brother. He and Simon followed Jesus all their lives. What heroes!

A Real Hero

1. How can you be like Andrew? (By telling a brother or sister about Jesus.)
2. Are you a loving brother or sister?

[Andrew] first found his own brother Simon and said to him, "We have found the Messiah."

John 1:41

John the Apostle

The Man Who Was the Lord's Best Friend

It was the saddest day ever. Jesus was on the cross. Jesus' best friend, John, stood close to Jesus' mother. They were sad. Jesus asked John to take care of His mother. He wanted John to treat Mary as his own mother. He did. John was Jesus' best friend.

A Real Hero

1. Would you like to be Jesus' best friend?
2. How can you be Jesus' best friend?

Then He said to [John], "Behold your mother."

John 19:27

Mary Magdalene
The Woman Who Was a True Follower

Mary Magdalene was a true follower of Jesus Christ. She loved Him. She followed Him everywhere. Mary was sad when Jesus died. She visited His tomb in the garden. But Jesus' tomb was empty! She ran to tell His other followers. Jesus chose Mary as the first person to see Him alive again.

A Real Hero

1. Pretend you are Mary. What will you say to Jesus in the garden?
2. Ask an adult to help you plant a tree in your yard. Let it remind you of the garden where Jesus was buried.

Mary Magdalene came and told the disciples that she had seen the Lord.

John 20:18

Barnabas

The Man Who Was a People Booster

Barnabas was a man everyone loved. He made other people feel good. One time Barnabas sold some of his land. He gave that money to the apostles. They used it to help other Christians. Barnabas was a people booster! He was a real hero.

A Real Hero

1. Why was Barnabas a hero? (He helped people.)
2. You can be a people booster, too! Make a card for someone who needs to be cheered up.

Joses was also named Barnabas by the apostles, (which [means] Son of Encouragement).

Acts 4:36

Stephen
The Man Who Was a Powerful Preacher

Stephen was a brave Christian. He was also a great preacher. Some people did not like what he said. They wanted to kill him. Stephen still preached the Word of God. One day a crowd threw stones at Stephen. He died. He was a hero because he loved God more than he loved himself.

A Real Hero

1. Find a small stone. Use it to remember how much Stephen loved God.
2. How can you be like Stephen? (By bravely telling others about Jesus.)

Stephen . . . did great wonders and signs among the people.

Acts 6:8

Philip

The Man Who Was a Traveling Teacher

An angel told Philip to go to the city of Gaza. On the way to Gaza, Philip met a man in a chariot. The man was reading God's Word. He asked Philip to help him understand it. Philip taught the man about Jesus. He also taught him how to be saved. The man was baptized. Then he was happy!

A Real Hero

1. Why was Philip a hero to the man in the chariot? (He told him how to be saved.)
2. Pretend to drive a chariot on the way to Gaza.

Then Philip . . . preached Jesus to him.

Acts 8:35

Dorcas

The Woman Who Was a Good Neighbor

Dorcas was a kind woman. She made coats to keep her neighbors warm. People loved Dorcas. One day Dorcas got sick and died. All the people she had helped were upset. God helped Peter bring Dorcas back to life. Then the people were happy. Dorcas was their hero.

A Real Hero

1. Draw a picture of a coat you would like to wear. Color it with your favorite colors.
2. Write a note to thank someone who did something nice for you.

Dorcas . . . was full of good works and
charitable deeds which she did.

Acts 9:36

Cornelius
The Man Whom God Heard

Cornelius was an important army leader. He loved God. He was kind. He gave gifts to others. He prayed to God often. One day God heard Cornelius' prayer. He sent an angel to Cornelius. The angel told Cornelius to send for Peter. When Peter came, Cornelius and his family were all saved.

A Real Hero

1. Ask an adult to help you write a letter to God. Thank Him for hearing your prayers.
2. Sing "Thank You, Lord" with someone.

[Cornelius] . . . who feared God . . .
gave . . . to the people, and prayed to
God always.

Acts 10:2

Lydia

The Woman Who Was the First Believer in Europe

One day Paul went to the river. He saw some women praying. He sat down to teach them. One woman was Lydia. She sold purple cloth to make a living. God helped her believe Paul's preaching. She was saved and baptized that day. She was the first person saved in Europe.

A Real Hero

1. Why was Lydia a hero to God? (She was the first believer in Europe.)
2. Pretend you sell purple cloth. How will you get people to buy it?

Lydia . . . was a seller of purple . . . .
The LORD opened her heart to heed the
things spoken by Paul.

Acts 16:14

Priscilla
The Woman Who Was a Partner in Truth

Priscilla and Aquila were wife and husband. They were partners for God. Apollos came to preach in their town. He was a great speaker. He taught God's Word the right way. But there were some things Apollos did not know. So Priscilla and Aquila taught Apollos more about God's Word. Then others could be saved.

A Real Hero

1. Ask someone to be your partner. Tell someone about God.
2. Work with a partner to put together a jigsaw puzzle.

When Aquila and Priscilla heard him
[Apollos], they . . . explained to him the
way of God more accurately.

Acts 18:26

Paul

The Man Who Could Do Miracles

The apostle Paul was a great hero among God's people. He preached God's Word. He did many wonderful miracles. He healed sick people. He helped people who were crippled walk. He helped people who were blind see. He also wrote many books of the Bible. Many people learned about Jesus from Paul. They were saved. He was a great man of God.

A Real Hero

1. God loves you as much as He loved Paul. What will you do for God?
2. What can you do to help a person who needs it?

Now God worked unusual miracles by the hands of Paul.

Acts 19:11

Titus

The Man Who Was a Helper and Comforter

The apostle Paul was tired. He had been through hard times. There were fights all around him. He needed to rest. God sent Titus to Paul. Titus took care of Paul. He helped him in many ways. He told Paul all the good news from his friends. Titus comforted Paul.

A Real Hero

1. Ask an adult to take you to see someone who needs to be comforted.
2. Do something nice to help your mom or dad right now.

God . . . comforted us by the coming of
Titus.

2 Corinthians 7:6

Timothy

The Man Who Was a Truth Protector

Timothy was a young preacher. He traveled with Paul. They were close friends. Paul thought of Timothy as his son. Later, Paul wrote a letter to Timothy. He told Timothy to protect the truth of God's Word from false teachers. God gave Timothy important work to do for Him. He was a true hero.

A Real Hero

1. Write a letter to your minister. Ask your minister to protect the truth of God's Word.
2. Sing "The B-I-B-L-E" with someone.

The glorious gospel of the blessed God
. . . was committed to my trust.

1 Timothy 1:11

Additional copies of this book
and other books in this series are available
from your local bookstore.

My Very First Book of Bible Fun Facts
My Very First Book on God
My Very First Book of Bible Lessons
My Very First Book of Prayers
My Very First Book of Bible Questions
My Very First Book of Bible Words
My Very First Book of God's Animals

If you have enjoyed this book, or if it has
impacted your life, we would like to hear from you.
Please contact us at:

Honor Kidz
Department E
P.O. Box 55388
Tulsa, Oklahoma 74155
Or by e-mail at info@honorbooks.com